SECOND EDITION

Storybook 15

The
Wind-up Book

by Sue Dickson

**Illustrations by Norma Portadino, Jean Hamilton,
Chip Neville and Kerstin Upmeyer**

Printed in the United States of America

Copyright © 1998 Sue Dickson
International Learning Systems of North America, Inc.
St. Petersburg, FL 33716

ISBN: 1-56704-525-1 (Volume 15)

C D E F G H I J K L M N—CJK—05 04 03 02 01 99

Table of Contents

Raceway Step 29   **Page**

| long ī | **Help the Blind** . . . . 3 |

by Lynda MacDonald

| u=ŏŏ air ui=ōō | **A Fair Day, A Bad Day** . . . . 9 |

by Vida Daly

Raceway Step 30

| or=er | **Mayor ? Janitor ? Doctor ?** |
What Will You Be? 14

by Rick Pantale and Sue Dickson

| Contractions |

Don't We Have Any Ice Cream ?   25

by Sue Dickson

| āré | **A Flat Tire and a Good Spare** . . . 30 |

by Vida Daly

| ä | **Buzzy Wasp Finds Something** . . . 37 |

by Sue Dickson

| c=s | **The Prince of France** . . . . 44 |

by Hetty Hubbard

Help the Blind

Vocabulary

1. blind

2. find

3. grind

4. wind

5. wind-up

6. kind

7. behind

8. mind

<u>Story Words</u>

pē⌀ ple
9. people

be tween
10. between

The blind man keeps a
  dog at his side.
The dog helps him find
  his way.
He helps him wind his
  way between
The people every day.

4

It is kind to help the
   blind
Cross with the traffic light.
The kind do not mind
   helping the blind,
For the blind man's day is
   night.

When you see a man
  who's blind,
Do not stay behind him.
You will learn from him,
  you'll find,
So, say "hello," and step
  beside him.

I'm tired of my toys.
I wish Dad would let
me have new ones.

I wish I had
a bigger bike.

He will teach you
to be glad –
Not sigh for things
you wish you had.

7

It is good to keep in mind...

We can learn **much** from the blind.

8

The End

A Fair Day, A Bad Day

Raceway Step 29
u=o̯o̯
air
ui=o̅o̅

Vocabulary

1. bushy
2. cushion
3. Butch
4. bull
5. pudding
6. full
7. pull
8. fair
9. chair
10. air
11. hair
12. stair
13. pair
14. nuisance
15. fruit
16. juice
17. suit

It was a fair day so Tim went outside to sit in his chair. He took a good book with him. His mom called him back to close the door.

A squirrel with a bushy tail was on Tim's chair. It ran away when it saw Tim coming, but it left a mess of nut shells for him to clean up!

Butch is a bull. Butch likes to sit on a cushion and eat at the table.

Butch likes to eat pudding ! Butch likes to put cream on his pudding.

Butch will eat till he is full.

Butch is a silly bull.

The book Tim took with him is called <u>Butch, the Silly Bull</u>.

"I like to put cream on my pudding, too," said Tim.

The air was blowing
Tim's hair. That was a
nuisance. It made it hard
for him to read. So he
went in to get some fruit
juice.

12

When Tim came out, he
tripped on the stair and
spilled the juice ! It
splashed on his suit and his
new pair of shoes ! What
can I say ? Tim had a
bad day ! Have you ever
had a bad day ?

The End

Mayor? Janitor? Doctor? What Will You Be?

Vocabulary

1. worth
2. worthy
3. mayor
4. author
5. sailor
6. janitor
7. elevator
8. operator
9. error
10. mirror
11. pastor
12. harbor
13. honor
14. worship
15. doctor
16. worry
17. world
18. work
19. word
20. actor
21. motor
22. neighbors
23. favor
24. color

14

What do you want to be when you grow up ? Do you want to be a mayor ?

Or do you want to be an author,

15

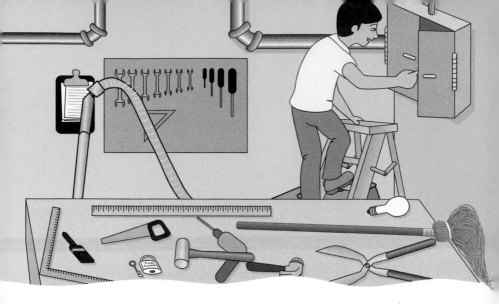

or a janitor,

or an elevator operator ?

Think about it and make no error. Look at yourself in the mirror and say, "I will choose to do something I enjoy."

Do your job well, and think about this: **It's nice to be important, but it's more important to be nice !**

17

Would you like to be a conductor and play music along the way?

Or work in a harbor
fixing motor boats
each day ?

19

You could be a mayor
and help make the laws.

Or you could be a sailor
and watch out for sharp

jaws !

If you are an author,
you'll see your name on
banners !

And when you are a visitor, you'll try to use your best manners !

Or if a doctor
   you choose to be,
When I get sick,
   you can take care of me!

23

Make it something you like,
whatever you choose,
For if you like it
that's very good news!

24   **The End**

Don't We Have Any Ice Cream ?

Vocabulary

1. do not . . . . .don't
2. are not . . . . . .aren't
3. I am . . . . .I'm
4. we will . . . . . .we'll
5. can not . . . . . .can't
6. we are . . . . . .we're
7. I will . . . . . . .I'll
8. did not . . . . . .didn't
9. it is . . . . .it's
10. have not . . . .haven't
11. you are . . . . .you're

Story Word

12. none

"Don't we have any ice cream?" asked Jeff. He looked into the freezer and there was none, just an empty space.

Mom called from the next room, "Aren't there some popsicles, Jeff?"

"They're not in here and I'm hungry!" said Jeff.

"I'm going to the store soon. You can come if you'd like, Jeff. We'll get some ice cream then," called Mom.

"I can't go with you, Mom. We're playing a ball game soon," said Jeff. "I'll be late for it if I go with you."

"Maybe you'd like Jello, Jeff. There's some on the top shelf. Look and see," called Mom again.

"Yes, said Jeff. "It's here, Mom! Mmm! I haven't had Jello in a long time! You're nice, Mom. Thanks!"

The End

A Flat Tire and a Good Spare

Raceway
Step 30B
āre

Vocabulary

1. fare
2. care
3. dare
4. bare
5. flare
6. spare
7. share
8. stare
9. rare

Have you ever had a flat tire? We did. We had just paid our fare at the toll booth, when...

Bump bump! Bump bump!

"Oh, no!" said Dad.

"Take care," said Mom. "We don't dare stop here. Let's get to the side of the road."

When Dad got off the road, Mom said, "Put on your sneakers, Robby. You can't help Dad in bare feet."

Dad lit a flare so the other cars could see us. He took the spare tire from the trunk.

Dad said I could help. It made me feel good to share the work.

"Look, Robby," said Dad. "There's the cause. This tire is bare and worn. I did not check it before we started. That's rare for me."

People stared at us as they drove by, but we didn't care.

A state trooper stopped
to help us. "We thank
you very much," said
Dad.

As we started for home,
Dad said, "It was good
of him to care. Wasn't
that nice?"

The End

Buzzy Wasp Finds Something

Vocabulary

1. wasp
2. wasps
3. father
4. swamp
5. Aha!
6. watch
7. watched
8. wanted
9. wash
10. washed
11. wad
12. watt
13. Ha ha!

Once there was a little
wasp named Buzzy. He
lived by a big swamp.
All day Buzzy watched
his father as he worked.

Father Wasp would fly across the swamp. He would dive to get a little wad of leaves or a dab of mud. Buzzy wanted to help Father Wasp but Father said,

39

"Go play with the other little wasps until you get bigger."

Buzzy flew across the swamp to play in the mud. Suddenly he saw something round and smooth under the mud!

"Oh, Father," called Buzzy. "I've found something that is like the moon! It must have fallen into our swamp."

"Come help me, Father! Help me get the moon out of the swamp."

41

Father flew to Buzzy. The thing that Buzzy found was as round as the moon and it was muddy and dirty. Father and Buzzy washed and washed it with swamp water. Was it really the moon ?

Then Father Wasp began to laugh, "Ha, ha, ha ! Buzzy, we have found something that is as round as the moon. Once it did shine, too, but it is just an old 100-watt light bulb !"

The End

The Prince of France

Vocabulary

1. prince
2. France
3. peace
4. rejoice
5. celebration
6. center
7. race
8. raced
9. city

10. fancy
11. cider
12. dance
13. circle
14. concert
15. face
16. voice
17. since

Story Word

18. clothes

Proclamation of a Celebration for Peace in France

France was having peace after a long war. The prince of France was happy. He wanted to make his people happy, too.

The prince said, "Let us rejoice and be glad. We will have a celebration !"

People raced to the center of each city. They had no fancy clothes, but they didn't mind. There was cider for all to drink and dancing for all to enjoy.

Bless our native land; there's peace in all of France. . .

There were concerts in the parks. Every face looked happy. Voices sang and hearts were glad.

The prince was glad his people were happy again.

The End